Life With Prayer Is A Life Worth Living!

Brandon Jack, Sr.

Edited by Kimberly Curtis
Cover designed by Devin Grey

Kingdom Publishing, LLC
1350 Blair Drive, Suite H-1
Odenton, Maryland 21113
www.kingdompublishingllc.com

Printed in the U.S.A
First Printing: 2017

ISBN 978-1-947741-01-0

ACKNOWLEDGEMENTS

I would like to thank my Heavenly Father, my wife (Katrina Jack), my two beautiful children (Brandon Jr and Logan), my family and church family without whose help this book would never have been completed. I want to specifically acknowledge Tonya Peterson for her editorial review, my father-in-law and pastor Kevin Hammond for his willingness to write my forward, and Devin Grey for designing the cover for this book as well as my website. I also want to thank Kingdom Publishing, LLC for all your help in getting this book published and available for readers.

Thank you all for your patience and guidance through this process of creating a book that will motivate people to spend quality time in prayer with God. I pray that this book will help encourage, stimulate, and speak to everyone who reads it.

Thank you Jesus Christ for being the living example of how we can be selfless and help save a nation consumed by sin.

I want to thank my beautiful wife for keeping me motivated during the writing and editing process of this book, you kept me encouraged when I felt the walls of idleness surrounding me. God knew I needed you in my life to keep me encouraged at times when I just felt like throwing in the towel. I love you baby!

FOREWORD

During the fall of 2015, a woman lay in the clutches of death. For this is what she and her family anticipated after a long hard-fought battle with a terminal illness. Nevertheless, there was something different about the outcome. Though this Woman of God labored with the symptoms and the finality of her plight, she clung to the very essence of a power that had been forged within her being from days gone by. This influence manifested itself within the room creating an atmosphere of peace for those left behind. Prayer and supplication had proven to be essential throughout her life. In her final moments suspended between earth and heaven, prayer was the bridge connecting her to God and His Kingdom. She exhaled her final breath on this side of glory to take her next in the land of promise; heaven.

It is prayer that unites the life of a believer with their Creator, bridging the chasm of our earthly dwelling to an eternal place; a land flowing with milk and honey. Prayer brings peace to the troubled mind, hope where hopelessness reigns, and power to the feeble heart. It is the conduit connecting the imperfect with perfection.

In this book, "Life With Prayer Is A Life Worth Living!" the author will take the reader on an intriguing and informative journey to discover the true power that can only be released through the art of prayer.

May God bless this book and add a blessing to the reader...

Kevin L. Hammond
Founder & Senior Pastor
13th Disciple of Christ Church
Chesapeake, VA

CONTENTS

PREFACE

One day in May 2015 while I was driving home from work in DC, I was in the midst of talking to God in prayer, praying that our nation would be unified and that love would conquer all the violence in the world, when He gave me the idea of writing a prayer book. My family and friends know that writing is not one of my interests. However, prayer is something I believe is very important. Prayer has gotten me through a lot of hardships. I have seen the manifestation of my prayers firsthand many of times throughout my life. I know how important prayer is in developing a relationship with God. Therefore, I opened myself up to the idea of writing.

After praying more about what God wanted from me for this book, I began to go through my Bible and select scriptures that stood out to me. Once I had a handful of scriptures, I began meditating on these scriptures and writing a prayer for each one, based on what I felt God was leading me to write. Then one day during my prayer time, God revealed to me the book title, the idea of a pocket style book, and the number of prayers to include.

I hope this book touches as many people's lives as possible, by introducing or reconnecting people to Jesus Christ through prayer.

I pray God speaks to you during your reading and prayer time. I believe this book will be a catalyst in further developing your relationship and spiritual growth with God. I pray He evokes a change, impacting your thoughts and your heart. Once He changes our thoughts, it will cause a change in our hearts which will consequently change our lifestyle.

If this book affects your life in a positive way, I encourage you to recommend this book to others in your life, in hopes that it will strengthen their relationship with God as well.

God bless,
Brandon Jack

ANGER

Deliverance

Don't be quick to fly off the handle. Anger boomerangs. You can spot a fool by the lumps on his head.
Ecclesiastes 7:9 (MSG)

Lord I pray out to you on my knees, because I need your help Father for I struggle constantly with my anger. It seems the more I pray for the chains to be broken the more things arise in my life to upset me. When those things come up I don't think of them as a test, therefore I continue to fail them. So Lord I am asking that you help me in the midst of my anger moments to remember this scripture. For I do not want to be labeled as a fool because I continue to operate out of my emotions, mainly anger. Lord I thank you right now for the deliverance of my anger and giving me joy and peace Lord. Thank you Father for all your help, Amen!

Emotions

Go ahead and be angry. You do well to be angry—but don't use your anger as fuel for revenge. And don't stay angry. Don't go to bed angry. Don't give the Devil that kind of foothold in your life.
Ephesians 4:26-27 (MSG)

Father God, help me with my feelings of anger and frustration. I no longer want to have these emotions. Lord when I begin to feel anger trying to creep up in my body, help me to operate in my spirit and put anger under subjection. Allow me to never let anger carry over from one day to the next. I do not want to leave any room for the devil to try to take foothold in my life. Please remove the spirit of anger and frustration from my body right now. I believe it and declare that spirit must go and never return. In the name of Jesus it is so. Amen!

COMMUNICATION

Thanksgiving

I love the LORD because he hears my voice and my prayer for mercy. Because he bends down to listen,
Psalms 116:1-2 (NLT)

Lord so many people forget that prayer is the easiest step to growing in their relationship with you. For me this is one area that is my strong suit, I love praying to you throughout the entire day for not only my needs, but standing in the gap by praying for those around me. I love you Father and thank you for bending down to listen to what I have to say. Thank you for answering my prayers in so many different areas of my life. No one will ever be able to tell me that you are not real; I know you are. We have conversations daily and I have seen the manifestation of my prayers. Thank you for hearing my voice and so many others. I have seen firsthand the power of prayer changing situations instantaneously. Amen!

Communication

Supplication

*Hear my voice when I call, Lord; be merciful to me and
answer me.*
Psalms 27:7

Oh Heavenly Father, I come to you to ask that you hear
my cries for help. I know that you stated in your word
that the prayers of the righteous are not forsaken.
Despite all my faults and issues I know that you still hear
me, because if you did not care to hear me then you
would have never sent your son Jesus Christ to die for a
broken world. Lord I know I am undeserving of salvation
and your grace and mercy, but I am so grateful that you
love me enough to extend grace and mercy to me. So I
ask that you please extend your ear down to hear my
requests for your help through these valleys that I am
facing right now. I know this is part of my journey to
grow in you, so I thank you for my valleys Lord. Amen!

FAITH

Healing

Now faith is confidence in what we hope for and assurance about what we do not see.
Hebrews 11:1

I declare healing in my life and the lives of my family who are going through health complications right now; that by the mighty name of Jesus we are healed and restored. I speak healing of any ailment, sickness or disease that is trying to take root in us and say that it cannot come back anymore. I declare that any broken bones and fractures, pains, or any other bodily injury and issue be healed right now, in the name of Jesus! I loose healing right now over my body and over my family, since you said in your word anything I loose on earth shall be loosed in heaven. So I know that by doing so you are already working spiritually to manifest the healing my family and I need. I thank you now for all these things and seal this prayer in Jesus name, Amen!

Faith

Freedom

Therefore I tell you, whatever you ask for in prayer, believe that you have received it, and it will be yours.
Mark 11:24 (NLT)

Lord I speak peace over my life, especially when I feel that everything around me is in utter chaos. Refresh and gladden my spirit. Purify my heart. Intensify my power. I lay all my affairs in your hand because you are my guide and refuge. I will no longer be sorrowful and grieved; I will be happy and joyful God! I will no longer be full of anxiety, nor will I let trouble harass me. I will not dwell on the unpleasant things of this life God, but focus on your goodness and the promises in your Word. I thank you right now for these things. Until we speak again I just praise your holy, matchless and wonderful name God. Amen!

Unbelief

*Wait patiently for the Lord. Be brave and courageous. Yes,
wait patiently for the Lord.*
Psalms 27:14 (NLT)

Lord I am struggling with waiting and being patient. I
trust you Lord but do not understand why my prayer
requests haven't been answered. Help me to overcome the
area of unbelief in my life. It is a small percentage
compared to my belief and faith in you, but it feels like it
takes control occasionally. Remove it from me
immediately; in the name of Jesus I proclaim it gone.
Lord I thank you for replacing my unbelief with even
more belief. Now I can be happy knowing that waiting
on you is the best thing for me, since you know exactly
the right time to answer my prayer requests. Amen!

Faith

FEAR

Strongholds

"So do not fear, for I am with you; do not be dismayed, for I am your God. I will strengthen you and help you; I will uphold you with my righteous right hand."
Isaiah 41:10

God, I need strength and help that only you can provide me with. At times, my fears and worries fill my mind and thoughts which prevent me from fully living the life you said I could have. I know your word is true and was written for me and all believers. So Lord please help me to get through this phase in my life by breaking the strongholds and chains of fear and worry. I also know that according to Jeremiah 29:11 you said that you have plans to prosper me and give me hope and a future. I thank you for breaking the chains of bondage over my mind when it comes to fear and worry and prospering me for a brighter future. I declare all these things done right now in Jesus name. Amen!

Worry

Such people will not be overcome by evil. Those who are righteous will be long remembered. They do not fear bad news; they confidently trust the Lord to care for them.
Psalm 112:6-7 (NLT)

God I thank you for everything that you have done for me; at times I forget the many blessings you have given me and what you have brought me out of throughout my life. I want to walk boldly in your Spirit Father; I no longer want to walk or operate with the spirit of fear. I know that I walk in righteousness, so I confidently trust you with my life. I will no longer fear things that would normally cause me to worry or get scared. For you allowed Peter who was all flesh to walk on water with Jesus; when Peter took his eyes off of Jesus he began sinking. Help me to keep my blinders on and stay focused on Christ and represent Him every day I have on this earth! I thank you right now, Amen!

Change

For the Spirit God gave us does not make us timid, but gives us power, love and self-discipline.
2 Timothy 1:7

God I know you have not given me the spirit of fear, so why am I afraid? At times I get fearful of change, which can cause me to be stagnate both naturally and spiritually. Lord help me to not be stagnate due to fear of change and fear of the unknown. Apply the necessary pressure in my life to direct me on the course you want me on, so I can fulfill the destiny you set forth for me. Allow your will and Holy Spirit to move me in all areas of my life. For change in my mind is too risky, but in you Lord there is no risk. In you, Father, I am safely kept. Amen!

FOCUS

Troubles

"So don't worry about tomorrow, for tomorrow will bring its own worries. Today's trouble is enough for today.
Matthew 6:34 (NLT)

Oh Father, help me to keep my focus on you each and every day. Help me to not focus on the troubles from yesterday or what is to come tomorrow and days down the road in my life. Help me to focus on getting through today and making the right decisions to grow and mature in you. Lord if I stumble and fall today, I ask you to remind me to get back up and keep on pushing and running my race. I know that in all of my stumbling you were there pushing me when my flesh did not want to press on. You are good all the time Father. Even when my life is in chaos you are still good and always will be. Nothing is too hard and big or too easy and small for You. You help me through my days and help keep my focus on Christ. I thank you now for all these things and seal this prayer in Jesus name, Amen!

Focus

Vision

My eyes are always on the LORD, for he rescues me from the traps of my enemies.
Psalms 25:15 (NLT)

Oh Lord, so many times I get so consumed in my own ways and emotions that I forget to keep my eyes focused on you, when you alone are my strength and way maker. When Peter had his eyes on Jesus, he was able to walk on water. As soon as he took his eyes off Jesus and began focusing on his surroundings he instantly started to sink. I know that You did not put that verse in the bible as just a story with no meaning, for every verse has meaning. So Lord please help me to keep my eyes on You and stop focusing so much on my surroundings, capabilities, wants, and emotions. I will be less prone to fall for the snares and traps of the enemy when I stay focused on You and stay in your presence Lord. I thank you now for all these things and seal this prayer in Jesus name, Amen!

FORGIVENESS

Falling Prey

If you are wise and understand God's ways, prove it by living an honorable life, doing good works with the humility that comes from wisdom.
James 3:13 (NLT)

Lord please help me not to stray away from your side because I don't want to fall victim to the temptations of this world; I want to honor you in everything that I do. Lord I ask that if I fall prey to temptation, become lazy or complacent that You will first forgive me of my sins and short comings. I ask you to speak to me, as only you know how to do, in order to get me centered and back in line with your way. I ask that you bless me with the wisdom you gave King Solomon. Forgive me Father for all the times I did not follow your commands but instead directly disobeyed you and ultimately dishonored you. I want to make you a proud Father and live the righteous life you have set forth for me. Amen!

Getting Even

Do not judge others, and you will not be judged. Do not condemn others, or it will all come back against you. Forgive others, and you will be forgiven.
Luke 6:37 (NLT)

Lord, I pray right now that you help me when it comes to having the mind set of wanting to pay people back who have wronged me. I do not want to be the one who comes to your gates and have you say that you do not know me because I have fallen into the cycle of getting even. Help me to be an encourager in the lives of others and to help promote them in the areas of weakness in their lives. Help me to uplift and guide them to the plan and purpose that you have for them. Help me to not judge others, but to instead pray for them when I notice they are doing something that goes against your Word. Help me to forgive those who have wronged me and in doing so it will cause a chain reaction of forgiveness. Thank you Lord for all these things, Amen!

GUIDANCE

Fork in the Road

Your word is a lamp to guide my feet and a light for my path.
Psalm 119:105 (NLT)

Lead me from death to life, from falsehood to truth. Lead me from despair to hope, from fear to trust. Lead me from hate to love, from war to peace. Let peace fill my heart, my local community, and this world. Lord Jesus, I ask you to give me all around peace in my mind, body, soul and spirit. I want you to heal and remove everything that is causing stress, grief, and sorrow in my life. Lord, guide my path through life and make my enemies be at peace with me. Let your peace reign in my family, at my place of work, at home and everywhere else I may go. Guide my hands to stay on the plow to do great works for the building of your Kingdom. Amen!

Finding the Exit

The thief's purpose is to steal and kill and destroy. My purpose is to give them a rich and satisfying life.
John 10:10 (NLT)

Lord God, I thank you right now for my life. Though my afflictions are great at times, I know that your plans are always for the prosperity and growth of your children. Even when I get off course or get caught in a trap from the enemy which is meant for death and destruction, you still provide a way of escape. By providing me a way of escape you allow me to grow and learn from my mistakes. Life is like a game of chess where we may deviate from the path you intended. But your all-knowing power guides us to make the next move towards getting back on track and hear your victorious words "Checkmate." This lets the dark forces of this world know they have been defeated. Amen!

How to Guide

"This, then, is how you should pray: "'Our Father in heaven, hallowed be your name, your kingdom come, your will be done, on earth as it is in heaven. Give us today our daily bread. And forgive us our debts, as we also have forgiven our debtors. And lead us not into temptation, but deliver us from the evil one.'
Matthew 6:9-13

Father God I thank you right now for your "how to guide" on prayer; for your Word shows me an example of how to pray unto you. I know that prayer is not about just speaking to you, or basically leaving you a voicemail in your inbox. I thank you for the connection and communication we have during my times of prayer with you Father. I know that all my prayers do not need to be long-winded, but what you require is prayer from a pure heart. I know that through prayer and fasting I can receive the full power of your Holy Spirit to go do the works you command me to do; to help save those who are lost. Thank you for your power, your guidance and direction. Amen!

HUMILITY

Docility

Then he turned to his host. "When you put on a luncheon or a banquet," he said, "don't invite your friends, brothers, relatives, and rich neighbors. For they will invite you back, and that will be your only reward. Instead, invite the poor, the crippled, the lame, and the blind. Then at the resurrection of the righteous, God will reward you for inviting those who could not repay you."
Luke 14:12-14 (NLT)

God thank you for providing so many examples in your Word about humility, and reminding me to stay humble. When I keep on the path of humility, it becomes such a great joy when I am able to help those whom I know could not repay me. The joy does not come from the mere fact that I am reaping my reward in heaven, but just because I am able to bring the love of Jesus into their lives and show them that someone cares about them. God help me to always be keen to your voice when you ask me to be a blessing to someone else. Give me that sense of guilt if I do not comply with the directions you have given me, so that I will not miss an opportunity to help someone in need. Amen!

Life Consumed

So humble yourselves under the mighty power of God, and
at the right time he will lift you up in honor.
1 Peter 5:6 (NLT)

Father, please help me. I more often than not am so consumed in my feelings and emotions that I forget why I am here in this world. I get so caught up in my job and in my personal life that I don't take the time to stop and give you all the glory and praise you deserve. If it were not for you saving me and keeping me, my life would be in shambles right now. I ask that you help me keep my focus on you and the reason you created me. I am here to help save a lost nation. When I am not under subjection to you, I lose my opportunity to help someone because I am so consumed in me. Lord I come to you kneeling at your feet asking for forgiveness. I humble myself before you. Thank you right now for helping me to humble myself under your mighty power, Amen!

JOY

Jubilance

*Joyful are those who obey his laws and search for him with
all their hearts.*
Psalm 119:2 (NLT)

Lord thank you for the joy you have given me; thank you
also for the pains and difficulties of this life. Without
having the bad days I would not truly appreciate my
good days. Most importantly every day is a great day
since you exhaled life into my body, allowing me to wake
up and see one more day. Help me to continue to obey
your laws and stay in constant meditation and prayer
with you, because I know in doing so you are filling my
spirit and bringing me a joy and peace that surpasses all
things of this world. Amen!

Treasure the Lord

Better to have little, with fear for the Lord, than to have great treasure and inner turmoil.
Proverbs 15:16 (NLT)

Oh Father how grateful am I that you have blessed me with all that I need. I know that these tangible things that I desire to have as my possessions while here on this earth will perish upon my death. I ask right now that you allow my heart, spirit and soul to align with your Holy Spirit. I have a fear of you Lord; I am not saying that I am afraid of you, but stating that I do not want to dishonor or disappoint you. I know in the Word that despite all the turmoil going on around me on the outside that I have peace and joy residing on the inside of me. Peace and joy which comes from you. Nothing can fill my heart and spirit with the peace and joy you provide Lord. I thank you for that right now, Amen!

LOVE

Agape

There is no greater love than to lay down one's life for one's friends.
John 15:13 (NLT)

Lord I thank you for your agape love that you have for your children. I did not deserve it, yet you sent your son Jesus Christ to live on this world and face the same tests I do. You knew I could not save myself or uphold the law, so you allowed your only son to die so I can have freedom from the bondage of sin. Lord I ask that you allow me to show your agape love to others. I want to bring lost souls to you, so they can experience the same relationship and love I have with you. Even if it means laying my life down for them or just being selfless and making time for others. Amen!

Covers All Things

*Most important of all, continue to show deep love for each
other, for love covers a multitude of sins.*
1 Peter 4:8 (NLT)

Wow God, this scripture sums up everything your son
Jesus Christ did for me. He showed his deep love for
humanity by suffering one of the most grueling and
painful forms of capital punishment ever created to give
us freedom of sin. Jesus' crucifixion was like a symphony
of pain created by every movement, with every breath;
even a slight breeze on his skin would have brought great
pain and distress. Lord please help me to always
remember all Jesus had to endure for me, so that when I
see someone in need of love I can show them your
unconditional love. Amen!

Sacrificial

Do nothing out of selfish ambition or vain conceit. Rather, in humility value others above yourselves.
Philippians 2:3 (NLT)

My human nature is to be selfish Lord, but you already knew I would focus on my issues at the expense of others. I am so thankful that you love me enough to send your son Jesus Christ to die for my sins and rise from the dead three days later to defeat death. In remembering that sacred sacrifice I cannot help but be humbled and work hard every day to live by the example of Jesus while living on this earth. I will value other's needs above my own. Remembering what you did for me, through the sacrifice of your only son Jesus, and what you continue to do every day when you extend your grace and mercy over my life. Amen!

Flourish

"For I know the plans I have for you," declares the Lord, "plans to prosper you and not to harm you, plans to give you hope and a future. Then you will call on me and come and pray to me, and I will listen to you. You will seek me and find me when you seek me with all your heart."
Jeremiah 29:11–13

Lord I thank you for your pleasant reminder in your Word that if I seek you with all my heart that I will find you Lord. Thank you for your promises to prosper me, listen to my calls to you, and to be ever present when I seek you. Your love for me is so great that it is hard to understand why you still love me when I continually do wrong and sin daily. I am so very grateful for your love, mercy, and grace that you extend to me. I promise to work harder at showing that same love to others. Amen!

It Only Takes One

"If a man has a hundred sheep and one of them wanders away, what will he do? Won't he leave the ninety-nine others on the hills and go out to search for the one that is lost?"
Matthew 18:12 (NLT)

Lord thank you that you said in Genesis 18 that you would not destroy Sodom for the sake of ten righteous people. I believe that if Abraham asked if one righteous person was in Sodom that your response would have been that you would not destroy it for the sake of just one. Lord I thank you for sending your son Jesus Christ to be my living example of a true shepherd. Show me how to demonstrate your great love and compassion to those around me. I too, want to be a shepherd of lost souls. I want to help bring others to know of your goodness so they can experience what you have given me. I want you to take me to places where the world has written people off, so with your help I can save the lost and bring them to your marvelous light. Amen!

Love

Unyielding

He personally carried our sins in his body on the cross so that we can be dead to sin and live for what is right. By his wounds you are healed.
1 Peter 2:24 (NLT)

Father thank you for your son Jesus Christ coming and taking on the sins of a nation. When temptations come my way, help me to have a visual remembrance of what Jesus endured for me at Calvary on the cross. That way I will not fall into temptation but operate out of my spirit. In doing so it will help me praise my way through the tests and tribulations that I am presented with. Thank you Jesus for taking the most torturous and disrespectful death so that I can have freedom from sin and so I can be healed. I declare healing from all things in my life that are not of you, and declare it done by the blood of Jesus. Amen!

Inheritance

I pray that your hearts will be flooded with light so that you can understand the confident hope he has given to those he called—his holy people who are his rich and glorious inheritance.
Ephesians 1:18 (NLT)

Help me to always remember I am your inheritance, you knew who I was and what I was destined to be before the beginning of time. Fill my heart with love and your light so that I can be a beacon to others. Let me be like a lighthouse to bring vessels (souls), that are stuck in the storms of this life or blinded by the fog around them, and guide them to safety (Jesus) so they can avoid calamity. Lord I ask that my family and my heart and soul will come to know the plans you have for us. I pray that our experiences with places and people of faith will ultimately call us to God and not turn us off to faith. I pray that our souls become secure in your love that only your son Jesus Christ can bring us. I pray that we learn to defend ourselves with the sword of the spirit and that we will be positive influences on others around us who do not know of your love, faithfulness, grace, and mercy. Amen!

Love

PRAISE

Honor

Then King David went in and sat before the Lord, and he said: "Who am I, Sovereign Lord, and what is my family, that you have brought me this far?
2 Samuel 7:18

Father, I just want to show you the utmost love and gratitude for everything you have blessed me and my family with. I thank you for bringing me this far in life, for you have given me life when I deserved death. You gave me and showered me with love when I deserved rejection and abandonment. You sat around listening to my cries for help when I was down, and not only did you listen but you helped pick me up and give me a brighter path. I just want to say Thank You Lord! I know you sent shepherds to help me back when I was living in sin. And you continue to help me grow in my relationship with you now. So Father I pray that you send shepherds from all generations and walks of life, to be used to help lead children, students and people of all ages to Jesus Christ so they can develop a personal relationship with Him. Amen!

Humility

Praise the Lord! Yes, give praise, O servants of the Lord.
Praise the name of the Lord! Blessed be the name of the Lord
now and forever. Everywhere—from east to west—praise the
name of the Lord. For the Lord is high above the nations;
his glory is higher than the heavens.
Psalm 113:1-4 (NLT)

Lord I come seeking your holy discernment and help; I am eager to indulge on your goodness. I am not asking for anything from you Lord, just seeking to be in your presence and tell you how grateful I am for everything that you have done in my life. Thank you for bringing me through my storms, even when I was the one who started them. Your love keeps me motivated to endure the hardships that have been before me, that I am facing now and that I will be presented with in the future. If sorrows, hardships, pains, and loss are part of your plan for my life, then I will endure them knowing you will keep me through it all. I thank you for my life and apologize for not taking full advantage of every day. I want to glorify you and help bring others to your marvelous light. I thank you now for everything Father. Amen!

Greatness

Tremble, O earth, at the presence of the Lord, at the presence of the God of Jacob. He turned the rock into a pool of water; yes, a spring of water flowed from solid rock.
Psalm 114:7-8 (NLT)

God I thank you for creating me and stating that mankind is more valuable than anything else you created during the seven days of creation. Father, the next time I observe the power of an ocean wave or the majesty of a mountain peak, help me to remember that your greatness and glory far exceed these natural wonders. You make mountains tremble at your presence alone. Knowing you are alive in me, I ask that you help me make this earth tremble to help bring those who are lost to you. I know trembling at your presence does not mean I am a coward or terrified, but that I am showing you that I recognize your complete power and authority and understand my frailty by comparison. I thank you right now for these things Lord. Until we speak again I just praise your wonderful name. Amen!

Thankful

Come, let us sing to the LORD! Let us shout joyfully to the Rock of our salvation. Let us come to him with thanksgiving.
Psalms 95:1-2 (NLT)

Father I thank you right now for everything you have done in my life. I am so humbled and thankful when I think of all that you have done for me and brought me through. I cannot help but rejoice with thanksgiving knowing that I did not and still do not deserve the grace, love, mercy and favor you have shown towards me. I remember when I gave my life to you Lord; that day was the best decision I have ever made in my life. I thought living for this world was great until I found you and accepted Jesus as my Lord and Savior. Despite all the obstacles, turmoil, and chaos that come up from time to time, I would not change any of those things because they have helped me to mature. I bask in your presence, for you are my rock, my strong tower, and my refuge. For you have blessed me with so many things I did not deserve and I am so humbled, honored and grateful that you did! I thank you now for all these things and seal this prayer in Jesus name, Amen!

Confession

But as for me, I will sing about your power. Each morning I will sing with joy about your unfailing love. For you have been my refuge, a place of safety when I am in distress.
Psalms 59:16 (NLT)

Thank you Father for the ability to praise you and spread your goodness to others. You have brought me through so much that I cannot ever forget your grace, mercy and goodness. I will forever praise your name regardless of my circumstances or trials. For I know that praising you will cause confusion to the devil and his dark forces. In a world full of spiritual warfare I will use my praise to win the battles. I thank you for the times you kept me and shielded me from the destruction and danger that I was both aware and unaware of. If it was not for your protection and love for me I know I would not be here today. Thank you Heavenly Father for everything you have done for me and I seal this prayer in Jesus name, Amen!

PRIDE

Egotistic

People may be right in their own eyes, but the Lord examines their heart.
Proverbs 21:2 (NLT)

Father, allow me not to continue to fall prey to the spirit of pride; thinking that I am always right. Allow the spirit that you have given me to be convicted when my thoughts begin to take on the spirit of pride and justification. I am yours Father; purify my heart and mind. Just like gold goes through a refining and melting process to become purified; do so with me God. Thank you now for melting away everything, (emotional, physical, and spiritual), that is not like you that has attached itself to me. I declare freedom in Jesus name, Amen!

Pride

True Self-Worth

Pride leads to disgrace, but with humility comes wisdom.
Proverbs 11:2 (NLT)

Lord I come seeking your help for I find myself at times being boastful and prideful throughout my days. I understand there is a fine line between pride and arrogance Lord, but I also understand that according to your word humility is the greater choice. So I ask you to help me be more humble in my life and how I go about my days. When people come in contact with me, they will not see me as prideful, but as humble and loving; they will see that I care for the wellbeing of those around me. I ask you to remove all traces of pride and fill me with humility, I declare it so in the name of Jesus Christ and thank you for this change. Amen!

Self-Glorified

*Not to us, O Lord, not to us, but to your name goes all the glory
for your unfailing love and faithfulness... The dead cannot sing
praises to the Lord, for they have gone into the silence of the grave.
But we can praise the Lord both now and forever!*
Psalm 115:1, 14-18 (NLT)

Father I ask for your forgiveness for I know that I have
come to you seeking to accomplish tasks in my life so
that I will be noticed. I failed you by not taking
advantage of giving glory and honor where it is due; to
you! Lord I do not want my concern for looking good or
impressing others to take precedence over your
reputation and your glory. So the next time I pray to you
for certain things, I will take time to cross examine my
request to see if you answered my prayer who would get
the credit. From this point forth I promise to give you all
the credit because you gave me everything. I have gifts,
talents, skills, and abilities. You are the one who created
me when I was hidden in my mother's womb. I thank
you now for all these things and will always make sure to
give you credit through my accomplishments Lord.
Amen!

Pride

PROTECTION

Protector

The name of the Lord is a strong fortress; the godly run to Him and are safe.
Proverbs 18:10 (NLT)

Father God, when I read this scripture I can't help but envision a young child frightened by an animal or noise and their immediate reaction is to run to their father for protection. Father I thank you for always being there in my times of need. When I have felt like life was too difficult to bear you were right there with your arms wide open calling me by name. I know I can run to you, any time of the day or night, for safety and protection from the evil in this world. Your protection is stronger than any man-made fortress or bomb shelter. Amen!

Protection

Shelter

"When you pass through the waters, I will be with you; and when you pass through the rivers, they will not sweep over you. When you walk through the fire, you will not be burned; the flames will not set you ablaze."
Isaiah 43:2

God I thank you for your word since it is a reminder that you will always be there with me and keep me. Despite how hard things seem during my trials and hardships I know you are always with me and you will never forsake me. At times I find myself so caught up in my trials and hardships that I forget what you said in your word; that those things will not be able to hurt me or overcome me. Lord I believe and have faith in you, that you can and will bring me through and out of my trials stronger, wiser and unscathed. I ask that you help me when I find myself in those moments of unbelief and when my flesh tries to reign over my spirit which you have given me. Thank you Lord for your protection through any storm that will come my way, Amen!

RELATIONSHIPS

Wife

The man who finds a wife finds a treasure, and he receives favor from the Lord.
Proverbs 18:22 (NLT)

Lord I thank you for my wife for she truly is my treasure from you Lord. I am thankful that you love me enough to give me such a wonderful blessing which is mine for a lifetime. Help me to be a better Godly husband and put her needs above my own, for in doing so I will please you. Not only will I please you Father, but it will also directly please my wife and be an example for those around us. Lord I know we may face good days and bad days, but I can truly say that I will never stop cherishing the wife you have given me. You gave man a wife to not only be a help mate in physical matters but most importantly in spiritual matters; to help lift me into the position you have called me to be. Amen!

Relationships

Husband

Wives, submit yourselves to your own husbands as you do to the Lord. For the husband is the head of the wife as Christ is the head of the church, his body, of which he is the Savior. Now as the church submits to Christ, so also wives should submit to their husbands in everything.
Ephesians 5:22-24

Lord I thank you for my husband for I know you've given him to me to be my guide through life. I need your help when it comes to fully submitting myself to my husband. So many times I do not agree with my husband's decisions and question his intentions. Lord I ask that you meet me where I am right now. Please open my heart and mind to be submissive to my husband as I am submissive to you. Convict me when the thought comes into my head that says my husband needs to earn my submission. I do not want to violate your word Father. I want to serve you completely throughout my life and being submissive to my husband is one of your commands. I thank you now for your help and guidance, Amen!

Friends

There are "friends" who destroy each other, but a real friend sticks closer than a brother.
Proverbs 18:24 (NLT)

Lord I thank you for not allowing me to fall into the repetitive cycles of this world, but to be set apart from them and follow your will. Allow me to help others who are complacent and stagnant in these cycles, specifically those whom I call or refer to as my friends. Lord, allow your light that is inside me to shine bright so that it will cause their lives to be changed forever; opening up their eyes to you and your Word. Help me to be a sibling to my friends, to always be willing to listen, and to help motivate and encourage my friends when they are in need. Amen!

Family

But if serving the Lord seems undesirable to you, then choose for yourselves this day whom you will serve, whether the gods your ancestors served beyond the Euphrates, or the gods of the Amorites, in whose land you are living. But as for me and my household, we will serve the Lord."
Joshua 24:15

Father, I ask that you shine your light upon my entire family. Give us the strength to overcome every stronghold, trial, tribulation, and difficulty we are dealing with now, and protect us against everything we may encounter throughout our lives. Father, please bring us all closer together and use us for your glory. May the love that binds us only grow stronger and more resilient as we fulfill the destiny you have laid out for each of us! Lord I ask for forgiveness for any and all sins we have committed knowingly and unknowingly. Soften our hearts so that we may also forgive one another Lord, as it is sometimes difficult to do. Help us to walk in unity so we can spread your gospel of the Kingdom to the nations. I thank you now for all these things and seal this prayer in Jesus name, Amen!

REPENTANCE

Gossip

Perverse people stir up contention; gossip makes best friends into enemies.
Proverbs 16:28 (VOICE)

God you know my heart wants to please you but I find myself at times partaking in gossip with others whether it is my coworkers, friends, classmates or family. Lord I know you do not approve of gossip for it leads to destruction. So I'm asking you to remind me of this scripture when I'm presented with opportunities to gossip; that way I will no longer operate out of my flesh, but out of my spirit, and make the right decision to not partake. In doing so, I hope others notice the change and ultimately invoke a change in their lives as well to stop partaking in gossip. I thank you right now for these things Lord, until we speak again I just praise your Holy, Matchless and Wonderful name God. Amen!

Repentance

Sin

...for you are still controlled by your sinful nature. You are jealous of one another and quarrel with each other. Doesn't that prove you are controlled by your sinful nature? Aren't you living like people of the world?
1 Corinthians 3:3 (NLT)

Father God, sin sure gets in the way when my spirit is trying to cooperate with your will. Sometimes I find myself just juggling sin and continuing to move through life like I work at the carnival. Lord I ask right now that you help me to realize how dangerous and detrimental this is in the spirit realm because I want to stay on the path of righteousness and not get caught up in a juggling act and straying from my destined course. I know that your word is true and that you say you have plans to prosper me and give me a future. So Lord help me to seek the way of escape when presented with sin. If I fall to sin help me to be repentant, stand up and continue down the path of righteousness. I thank you right now for all these things Lord; until we speak again I just praise your holy name God. Amen!

Safety

"Therefore you shall do my statutes and keep my rules and perform them, and then you will dwell in the land securely."
Leviticus 25:18 (ESV)
But God demonstrates his own love for us in this: While we were still sinners, Christ died for us.
Romans 5:8

Thank you for the law you gave Moses on Mount Sinai. Lord thank you for sending your son Jesus Christ to die for my sins for I am born with the desire to sin and not follow your laws. Only through acceptance of your Son as my Savior am I free of the bondage of sin and able to live in safety. My safety comes in the repentance of my sins, and my willingness to die to my flesh. Your Word is the light to my path and the lamp to my feet that guides me safely through this life. Your Ten Commandments are the rules that guide me safely on my journey. Thank you for making them since you designed them to protect me from harm and to keep me in line with your will. Most of all thank you for sending your son Yeshua to die on Calvary's cross for me. Now the shackles of sin are broken and all of your creation can live in freedom. Amen!

Stubbornness

"The rich man replied, 'No, Father Abraham! But if someone is sent to them from the dead, then they will repent of their sins and turn to God.' "But Abraham said, 'If they won't listen to Moses and the prophets, they won't be persuaded even if someone rises from the dead.'"
Luke 16:30-31 (NLT)

God help me to not be like the people referenced in this scripture for I do not need to see someone raised from the dead to repent of my sins or to prove that you are alive. I am a witness to all the great and wonderful things you have done in my life, big and small. I believe your Word and that Jesus came to earth and died for my sins. Therefore, Lord, help me to remember to repent daily so sin will not have a stronghold in my life. I'd still be bound to sin if it wasn't for your love; you allowed your son Jesus Christ to come thousands of years ago to give His life for my life, so that I could be free of sin. Oh thank you for that great act of selflessness and love and help me to be the "walking dead" for others to see that they can be loosed of their shackles of sin and walk in freedom. Amen!

Sacrifice

Give your burdens to the lord, and he will take care of you.
He will not permit the godly to slip and fall.
Psalms 55:22 (NLT)

Oh Lord so many times I feel like I have to come to you spotless and perfect, which makes me slow to ask for your help. I now understand that I will never be good enough and that is why you sacrificed your son Jesus Christ and allowed his blood to be shed for me and this world. I thank you for bleeding and dying for me Lord. I lay all my burdens at your altar Lord as a sacrifice so that I can rid myself of the things that are keeping me from fulfilling my destiny. I no longer wish to walk through this life blind and lost by not operating in my God given purpose that you created me to fulfill. I declare from this day forth that I will walk into my purpose and destiny that you have for me. Amen!

RESPECT

Considerate of Others

This is what our Scriptures come to teach: in everything, in every circumstance, do to others as you would have them do to you.
Matthew 7:12 (VOICE)

Father so many times I see on the television, internet, or newspaper about the total lack of respect for people on this earth. There are people in this world who are living by this scripture who perform good deeds in their everyday lives because they know you command it. Father I pray right now that this nation open its eyes to your word and begin to live their lives according to this scripture. My God how much more enjoyable life would be if everyone treated others the way they want to be treated. This is not a new phrase. Growing up you would always hear your parents and grandparents tell you to treat people the way you would want them to treat you. So Father I ask in the name of Jesus Christ that this nation have a conviction, that their hearts be conformed to yours, and that they will begin to treat others with love, respect, and kindness. Amen!

Respect

Reverence

Let us begin. The worship of the Eternal One, the one True God, is the first step toward knowledge. Fools, however, do not fear God and cannot stand wisdom or guidance.
Proverbs 1:7 (VOICE)

Oh Lord, I do have fear and respect for you Father just like any child would have for their parents. Lord I find myself trying to push back against your commands just like I did naturally when I was a child trying to test the limits with my parents. Father I ask you to help remove that mindset from me. I do not want to be a stubborn fool by refusing to respect you and not having reverent fear for you. For you are my Creator; you created the heavens and the earth with your words. So I know you can help me get myself in check when my flesh tries to act out. I thank you for that right now Father, Amen!

SALVATION

Sustentation

There is salvation in no one else! God has given no other name under heaven by which we must be saved."
Acts of the Apostles 4:12 (NLT)

Lord I know it is by you alone I am saved and have eternal life after accepting your son Jesus Christ as my Lord and Savior. I also know there are so many other religions on this earth that believe their "god" will keep them from destruction after they die; reincarnate them as an animal; or reward them with pleasures of the flesh. Yet I know you are the only true and living God because you keep me each and every day and I have seen your word come to life not only in my life but in the lives of those around me. So Lord I ask that you help use me to speak to anyone I know who may believe in a "false god and idol" and help show them your love so they can be saved by Jesus Christ. I do not want to see anyone perish and get sent to hell due to confusion, ignorance, or stupidity. I thank you now for all these things and seal this prayer in Jesus name, Amen!

Salvation

Godly Liberation

*"Or suppose a woman has ten silver coins and loses one.
Won't she light a lamp and sweep the entire house and
search carefully until she finds it? And when she finds it, she
will call in her friends and neighbors and say, 'Rejoice with
me because I have found my lost coin.' In the same way,
there is joy in the presence of God's angels when even one
sinner repents."*
Luke 15:8-10 (NLT)

Lord God thank you for saving me when I was living in sin, bound to the lifestyle of sin and seeking the pleasures of this world. Father you did not have to continue to work on getting me to open my eyes to accept your son Jesus Christ into my life, yet you loved me enough to keep pushing and allowing things to happen (good and bad) in my life to help me see the light! I know that not only was I rejoicing when I accepted your son Jesus into my life, but you and all of heaven were rejoicing along with me. Use me to be the vessel you created me to be; use me to help a sinner develop a repentant heart and accept your son Jesus as their personal savior. I thank you for choosing me to be your light carrier for others to see. Amen!

Seeking Redemption

If you openly declare that Jesus is Lord and believe in your heart that God raised him from the dead, you will be saved. For it is by believing in your heart that you are made right with God, and it is by openly declaring your faith that you are saved.
Romans 10:9-10 (NLT)

Oh righteous Father I declare that your son Jesus Christ is Lord of my life and I believe in my heart that three days after his crucifixion you raised him from the dead; giving Jesus dominion over death and the grave. I thank you right now for my free gift of salvation Father. I do not ever want to be separated from you. I eagerly want to see others in my life saved from condemnation. I pray that you help me to not be afraid of spreading this scripture to the nations, so that I can be used as a catalyst in someone's life to help them receive salvation and develop a relationship with you Lord. I thank you right now for the free gift of salvation and I forever praise you for your love and faithfulness. Amen!

SERVING

Selflessness

*Don't be selfish; don't try to impress others. Be humble,
thinking of others as better than yourselves. Don't look out
only for your own interests, but take an interest in others,
too.*
Philippians 2:3-4 (NLT)

Lord I thank you right now for taking away all selfish
ambition and replacing it with selflessness; for I want to
be used by you to help others I come in contact with in
my daily activities. Lord help me to slow things down
and not focus so much on myself but begin to focus on
how I can help someone else. Allow me to focus on
opportunities to bless others instead of how you can bless
me Lord. I thank you right now for using me to help a
multitude of people that I come in contact with
throughout my day (my neighbor, colleague, classmate,
etc.). Just send me a conviction when I pass over
someone in need, because of my own selfish mentality, so
that I can be used by you to help that person. For I am
your servant and I know your will and purpose are
perfect. I thank you now for all these things and seal this
prayer in Jesus name, Amen!

Listening Ear

Shoulder each other's burdens, and then you will live as the
law of the Anointed teaches us.
Galatians 6:2 (VOICE)

Sometimes I forget the impact of simply listening to someone pouring out their heart to me. When I listen to someone share their thoughts with me, I am helping carry the weight of the burdens they are suffering. I think about all the times I have poured out my heart to you and how you listened to my calls for help. In the midst of me pouring out my heart to you, you took the weight of my afflictions and placed them on your shoulders. I am so grateful to you for taking my weight away and for the people you placed in my life that have taken time to listen to me and help carry my burdens. Lord allow me to be used today as a listening ear for someone who is in need, so I can help carry the weight of their afflictions. Amen!

Purpose

Teach me to do your will, for you are my God. May your gracious Spirit lead me forward on a firm footing.
Psalm 143:10 (NLT)

Lord I thank you right now for keeping my footing firm in you and helping me to stay on the path of righteousness. Continue to teach me to follow your ways, your will, and your purpose for my life. I don't want to be a hindrance from what you want me to do each and every day, nor from bringing people to you and allowing them to experience the love of Jesus Christ. I ask you to open the eyes and ears of my heart to hear from you and see the plans you have for me each day, so I can be used to bless someone else. Amen!

Signs and Wonders

"And now they're at it again! Take care of their threats and give your servants fearless confidence in preaching your Message, as you stretch out your hand to us in healings and miracles and wonders done in the name of your holy servant Jesus."
Acts 4:29-30 (MSG)

Lord give me the boldness and power that is required to heal the sick and raise the dead by using the name of Jesus and having faith that it is already done. I understand that the only way I can receive the power and boldness is to first come into your presence by getting on my knees and entering into prayer with you. Throughout your word you give many examples of how your son Jesus would pray and fast before healing the sick, raising the dead or doing other signs and wonders throughout the nations. So Father help me to do the same, so that I may walk in the boldness and power to save people and bring them to Jesus. Amen!

Breaking Chains

So I turned to the Lord God and pleaded with him in prayer and fasting. I also wore rough burlap and sprinkled myself with ashes.
Daniel 9:3 (NLT)

Lord I want to spend this time to intercede on behalf of the world. Father I pray right now for repentance of sins that have been committed against you. I ask that you touch the hearts of those who are operating in sin so they can experience your forgiveness and ultimately the breaking of shackles. For I know that Jesus Christ came and already paid the penalty of sin through his death and that he defeated death through His resurrection. So I pray that those who are lost in the world will begin to seek after you like people seek for emergency supplies in preparation for weather emergencies. You gave me an eye opening experience that I am forever grateful for, because without it I'd still be living in sin. Lord I also ask you to continue extending your grace over their lives and give them the convictions necessary to help direct them down the path of righteousness. Thank you Lord, Amen!

Boldness

Then, to the others, "Go ahead, take away the stone." They removed the stone. Jesus raised his eyes to heaven and prayed, "Father, I'm grateful that you have listened to me. I know you always do listen, but on account of this crowd standing here I've spoken so that they might believe that you sent me."
John 11:41-42 (MSG)

Oh God thank you for this reminder that through my prayers I can have an intimate conversation with you. In this scripture Lord you are telling me that it is important to pray out loud to you. I know you can hear my prayers in my thoughts, but I believe you want me to pray aloud to keep my mind from wandering, so I can keep my focus on you. In keeping my focus on you, I will begin to grow spiritually. Most importantly praying out loud can strengthen and encourage those who happen to be standing around and listening. Lord help me to pray aloud through all circumstances regardless of where I am or who I am around, that way you can use my prayer to touch someone's heart and plant a seed of belief in their hearts. Amen!

Serving

Soften Hearts

For the Lord grants wisdom! From his mouth come knowledge and understanding. He grants a treasure of common sense to the honest. He is a shield to those who walk with integrity. He guards the paths of the just and protects those who are faithful to him.
Proverbs 2:6-8 (NLT)

Father, help me to stay faithful to you and to your word and help me to be honest and truthful all the days of my life. In doing so I know that according to your word you will shield me, you will guard my path, you will give me a treasure of common sense and you will protect me. I pray right now for those people in my life who I know have backslidden from you or those who have completely ignored you. I pray that you soften their hearts and open their minds to be receptive to your word and to your voice. Once they receive your word and begin listening to your voice, I pray they will seek after you and give their lives over to you. Once they do so I know you will protect them, guard their paths, shield them and give them a treasure of common sense. Amen!

Comforting Others

Praise be to the God and Father of our Lord Jesus Christ, the Father of compassion and the God of all comfort, who comforts us in all our troubles, so that we can comfort those in any trouble with the comfort we ourselves receive from God.
2 Corinthians 1:3-4

Lord, I ask that you allow me to be able to help comfort those who are currently dealing with trouble. I know it is only by your strength that I have made it through all my hurts, pains and discomforts. I could not have done it on my own because I was so ready to throw in the towel and quit on life. When troubles come my way now, I am able to rejoice through it all. Even when I look back over my life I know that it was all because of your grace, love and mercy. Please use me to be a blessing to others. I know you brought people into my life for a season, just to help me when I was in my time of need. Allow me to return the favor to others so they can experience the same joy I did when someone helped me to get through. I declare your will Father, not my will. Amen!

Standing in the Gap

The LORD is close to all who call on him, yes, to all who call on him in truth. He grants the desires of those who fear him;
Psalms 145:18-19 (NLT)

Lord I call on you right now seeking your strength and protection from my current circumstances. It seems like everything around me is quickly heading for destruction and going against your word. There is death all around me; Lord I fear your wrath and judgment for those who are not in relationship with you and have not accepted Jesus Christ into their lives. Please hear me as I pray that all hardened hearts will be broken and molded to your heart. I know you are coming soon and I do not want to see anyone perish due to their pride, arrogance, or lack of faith in you. I know the enemy is hard at work trying to capture the souls of those who are lost; I stand right now in the gap for them and pray by faith for a transformation of this nation. I pray that everyone will seek your salvation through your son Jesus Christ. I thank you now for all these things and seal this prayer in Jesus name, Amen!

Light Bearer

Jesus spoke to the people once more and said, "I am the light of the world. If you follow me, you won't have to walk in darkness, because you will have the light that leads to life."
John 8:12 (NLT)

Oh Lord I thank you right now for placing your glorious light inside of me and trusting me with your light. So many times when I am confronted with dark situations I forget that those things or people are only around because they see your light inside of me. Lord help me not to forget that I am holding your light inside of me and that I need to let your light shine everywhere I go so that others can get a glimpse of it and be changed forever. I want you to use the light inside of me to brighten the darkest areas, not only in my life, but in the lives of those around me. I want to be used by you Lord to help bring light, salvation, peace, and joy to others. I thank you now for all these things and seal this prayer in Jesus name, Amen!

Helping

Therefore, whenever we have the opportunity, we should do good to everyone—especially to those in the family of faith.
Galatians 6:10 (NLT)

Lord, so many times I find myself eager to help those less fortunate around me, and I know that pull and sense of urgency in certain matters is your holy spirit convicting and speaking to me. I ask you to help me continue to be alert to opportunities to help those in my day to day life. Lord, help me not to focus just on those outside in the world but also the individuals in my church whom are believers in you. You allowed people to help me when I was living in my sinful state, so I ask you to use me to be a blessing to someone else Father; especially to those in my church. I know there are probably people walking around with a mask on like everything is alright, yet their life is messed up or in shambles. So Father I ask you to help me to help them either by listening to their story, blessing them, or sharing my testimony with them. I thank you now for all these things and seal this prayer in Jesus name, Amen!

Changing the World

I urge you, first of all, to pray for all people. Ask God to help them; intercede on their behalf, and give thanks for them. Pray this way for kings and all who are in authority so that we can live peaceful and quiet lives marked by godliness and dignity.
1 Timothy 2:1-2 (NLT)

Father God I pray right now for all those who have power over the decisions of this country. Guide them to make just and right decisions and not to feel forced to make decisions based on others influences. Do not let them be deceived by the enemy to make a decision that does not line up with your will. Soften their hearts to be vulnerable to your word, guidance, love, and to live according to your will. I pray for their peace of mind and that you protect them from all the attacks they face on a daily basis, and help them overcome those attacks. Lord intercede on their behalf to guide them through their days. Lord I also pray the world will accept your will, and give their lives to you. I pray for their salvation and that you intercede on their behalf when they lose hope and strength Father. I thank you now for all these things and seal this prayer in Jesus name, Amen!

SPIRITUAL ANGUISH

Mourning

Blessed are those who mourn, for they will be comforted.
Matthew 5:4

Father God, I don't understand your ways or reasoning behind all the misfortune I have had in my life. But Lord I know you have a greater purpose for everything. I know according to your word that through my mourning I receive comfort and blessings that come only from you. For your word says that weeping and sorrow may last all night, but joy comes in the morning. Lord please heal my hurt and sorrow and help me to continue to trust you with my life when things do not make any sense to me naturally. Help my spiritual eyesight to show me the purpose you have for my sorrows. Thank you Father for all these things, Amen!

Quitting

I have told you all this so that you may have peace in me.
Here on earth you will have many trials and sorrows. But
take heart, because I have overcome the world."
John 16:33 (NLT)

Oh Father so many times I feel like calling it quits and wish you would just hurry up and call me to be with you, due to all the trails and sorrows I deal with. Your word always picks me back up and helps me remember you have overcome this world through the death and resurrection of your son Jesus Christ. Just keep this scripture close to my heart and mind when I am suffering trails, tribulations, and sorrows in my life so I will have the peace you said I can have. I know the enemy wants me to give up so that I do not fulfill the destiny you have given me. Yet I will continue to stand, spreading your glorious gospel of the kingdom and declaring your word. I thank you right now for these things Lord, until we speak again I just praise your matchless name God. Amen!

SPIRITUAL GROWTH

Success

Whatever you do, do it as service to Him, and He will guarantee your success.
Proverbs 16:3 (VOICE)

God I thank you that according to the Word, if I commit my actions and plans to you that you will cause them to be successful. Help me Father to remember to commit my plans to you first before trying to make them happen for myself. When I do forget to commit my plans to you please charge it to my mind, not to my heart, and forgive me Lord. I know you will use my forgetfulness as a teachable moment. And that teaching moment will only have a purpose to prosper me because you never have negative plans for your children. Amen!

Heart Issues

Trust in him at all times, you people; pour out your hearts to him, for God is our refuge.
Psalm 62:8

Lord, I know I can come to you with any situation and can vent to you with my struggles. You are a loving God who will not condemn me but you will listen and give me the peace only you can give. I cry out to you Father right now and ask you to remove the things that are heavy on my heart. Please give me peace and comfort right now to deal with the troubles and afflictions that are heavy on my heart. I trust you Lord and I trust that despite the way things seem carnally that you allow things to happen for my benefit and spiritual growth and maturity. Amen!

Foolishness

The first speech in a court case is always convincing—until the cross-examination starts!
Proverbs 18:17 (MSG)

Lord, allow me not to walk around as a fool, walking in blindness to the sin that still has me shackled up. I ask you to open my eyes so I can see the areas in which I struggle. Allow my mind and mouth not to justify these sins based off of the world I live in and what is acceptable to society. I know the only thing I need to use as justification is your Word. Lord I present my sin to you right now. In the name of Jesus Christ I declare that every chain of bondage be broken permanently. Allow me not to go with what society tells me, but to stick to your unfailing Word that is always true; it is my road map through this life on earth. Amen!

Spiritual Growth

Freedom of Bondage

There is a time for everything, and a season for every activity under the heavens; a time to tear and a time to mend, a time to be silent and a time to speak.
Ecclesiastes 3:1, 7

Lord, I thank you for your refining moments when you let me go through the fire so that I will be purified. My trials and struggles may have appeared to be a hindrance in my life, but I truly thank you for allowing those things to happen to me. I did not realize when I was going through them, what significance overcoming those struggles would have in my life. Now I see how they helped me grow and mature in my relationship with you by removing everything that was bound to me and did not line up with your will or your way in my life. Thank you for every season I am able to experience (good, bad or ugly) because it shows your love for me and that you are still equipping me for what lies ahead. Amen!

Training

"Physical training is good, but training for godliness is much better, promising benefits in this life and in the life to come."
1 Timothy 4:8 (NLT)

Lord, I know that exercise and healthy eating are important parts in having a healthy life and longer life expectancy. I ask that you help me not to forget the most important training that will give me benefits in this life and eternal life. This is the training of my spirit which comes by continuing to feed it with your Word, meditating on your Word, and fasting (from fleshly and worldly desires) to be closer to you; by spending quality time with you in prayer, and being a blessing to others. Father continue to help me stay in shape spiritually so that I can and will be ready for anything that is thrown at me. Amen!

Warfare

Finally, my brethren, be strong in the Lord and in the power of His might. Put on the whole armor of God, that you may be able to stand against the wiles of the devil. For we do not wrestle against flesh and blood, but against principalities, against powers, against the rulers of the darkness of this age, against spiritual hosts of wickedness in the heavenly places.
Ephesians 6:10-12

Even with all the attacks I face throughout my day; I know that the root cause of these attacks is spiritual warfare. I know that principalities of wickedness will try to gain access into the minds and hearts of people so they can corrupt them and cause the chaos that I see in this world to sky rocket. I pray that you continue to help equip me for battle because I am more than willing to put on the whole armor of God. Please open my eyes up to see these spirits of darkness that are afflicting people, so that I can speak to them and cast them away in the name of Jesus. Amen!

Correction

All Scripture is inspired by God and is useful to teach us what is true and to make us realize what is wrong in our lives. It corrects us when we are wrong and teaches us to do what is right. God uses it to prepare and equip his people to do every good work.
2 Timothy 3:16-17 (NLT)

Thank you for giving me your Word Lord, so I can use it as an instruction manual to navigate my way through this life and through all circumstances and situations that arise. I thank you for your correction, although I do not like to go through the correction process. I know that your correction will help me to make the right decisions and help prepare me and equip me for the spiritual warfare I will have to face each day. Help me to not fall into the repetitive cycles of this world; just going through the motions mindlessly, but help me to do what is right in a world full of wrong living. I want to stand out and cause others to notice the light of Christ in me so I can introduce them to your son by living a life that is representative of Him. Amen!

Finding My Identity

The earth is the Lord's, and everything in it, the world, and all who live in it; for he founded it on the seas and established it on the waters.
Psalm 24:1-2

Father I come before you humbly, seeking my true identity in you. I understand that every trial and tribulation I face is to help prepare me for the plans and destiny you have in store for me. Father I ask you to open up my heart and mind to be more vulnerable to your word and your will. Help me to truly understand the calling you have over my life. I want to live according to your purpose for me and not according to this world's limitation. Father God help me to grow in you so that I may have more wisdom, be more mature in you and serve you completely without excuses or delays. Lord, help me to use my praise and worship to glorify you and to help others find their identity in you. I thank you now for all these things and seal this prayer in Jesus name, Amen!

STAYING IN LINE

Eyesight

God is not human, that he should lie, not a human being, that he should change his mind. Does he speak and then not act? Does he promise and not fulfill?
Numbers 23:19

Lord I know I allow myself to look at life with my natural eyes which hinders me from being everything you want for my life. I allow circumstances, fears, and logic to spiritually blind me and physically hinder me along my path in life. Father I know my spiritual eyesight also ties into being spiritually minded so I ask you to help my spiritual mindset and eyesight to line up with your will and your way. I recognize that before I can ever accomplish anything meaningful in my life, I have to seek you to find out your will first, so I can see if my thoughts line up with what you have planned for my life. Amen!

Thoughts

I will climb up to my watchtower and stand at my guard post. There I will wait to see what the Lord says and how he will answer my complaint.
Habakkuk 2:1 (NLT)

Thank you for waking me up each day Lord. Allow my first thoughts of the day to focus on the fact you have placed me here for a purpose. It's important to start my day with faith and set my mind in the right direction. When I do I can then go out expecting your favor Lord. I want to start each day by asking myself what am I believing to happen that day. I ask you that when I get an answer to the question that you begin to reveal to me whether my belief is an authentic promise from you or just a fabricated wish. I do not want to operate out of fleshly desires, but instead I want to make sure my thoughts and ideas are spiritually guided and motivated. Thank you for your clarity which helps me stay in line and in tune with you Lord. Amen!

Secret Rooms

Who may ascend the mountain of the Lord? Who may stand in his holy place? The one who has clean hands and a pure heart, who does not trust in an idol or swear by a false god. They will receive blessing from the Lord and vindication from God their Savior. Such is the generation of those who seek him, who seek your face, God of Jacob.
Psalm 24:3-6

Lord I come to you asking that you help me to stop keeping the "secret rooms" in my life locked, or constraining your access. I forget and sometimes just ignore the fact that you are omnipotent and that you already know what I am trying to hide from you in the first place. Help me to be transparent with you and with myself. Help me to unlock these "secret rooms" and make the necessary changes so I can live upright and acceptable in your sight. I want my worship and my way of life to be a complete representation of you God, so that everyone around me will begin to encounter your light, power, greatness, and agape love. I thank you now for all these things and seal this prayer in Jesus name, Amen!

STRENGTH

Fitness

For I can do everything through Christ, who gives me strength.

Philippians 4:13 (NLT)

God thank you for being my El Sali, my rock and my strength. Help me to remember that when I am weak, you are right there to give me the strength I need to make it through. All I need to do is ask and believe in order to receive. Just like in physical fitness there are days of muscle fatigue after a workout. When I am being tested (going through my desert), I can stop and recognize that this is all part of the process of developing greater spiritual strength. Lord I thank you that in my weakness and fatigue you are always there for me; watching over me, and protecting me. Amen!

Strength

Adversity

This is my command—be strong and courageous! Do not be afraid or discouraged. For the lord your God is with you wherever you go.
Joshua 1:9 (NLT)

Father God, thank you for letting me know you are always here with me. Even when I ignore you and disregard what you ask me to do, you still stand by me. I am so sorry for not being attentive to what you ask of me at all times. I ask right now Lord that you give me the courage and strength to face the problems and strongholds that are currently trying to wreak havoc in my life. I know you do not allow things to come my way by circumstance but that every problem and stronghold I face has a greater purpose to help me to mature in you and grow into the masterpiece you created me to be. Amen!

Seeking Help

"O Sovereign Lord! You made the heavens and earth by your strong hand and powerful arm. Nothing is too hard for you!"
Jeremiah 32:17 (NLT)

God, help me with the areas of my life that seem impossible to overcome and help me to remember not to lose hope or faith when things seem too hard for me naturally. Help me to remember that nothing is too hard or impossible for you, all I must do is ask for your help in the middle of my storm and you will calm it just like your son Jesus Christ did in Matthew 8:23-27. Lord I want to thank you for all the examples I see every day that are a reminder of just how strong and powerful you are. Help me to slow down to really appreciate all you have given me and to see the world around me from a different perspective, that way I can appreciate all the examples of your greatness each day; they will help me to stay close to you and not give up any territory to the enemy. Amen!

Facing Fatigue

But the Lord is faithful; he will strengthen you and guard
you from the evil one.
2 Thessalonians 3:3 (NLT)

Oh God, I need you to fill me up with your spirit and allow it to overflow out of me. I am coming to you right now as an open and empty vessel ready to be poured into. Please give me the strength I need to endure all the trials and tribulations, and to help me pass the tests that you present me with. Father I no longer want to fail the tests you present to me. Help me to overcome all temptations, to have dominion over my flesh, and to place my emotions under subjection. Lord when the weight of this world and its issues try to weigh me down, I ask you to take those weights off of me and give me the strength to endure my trials. Father I ask you to guard me from the enemy and help me to outwit the devil just like Jesus did in the wilderness for 40 days and nights. Amen!

Equip Me for My Destiny

Don't you realize that all of you together are the temple of God and that the Spirit of God lives in you?
1 Corinthians 3:16 (NLT)

Thank you Father for your word which is a reminder of the things I can forget so easily when I am living in this world. I sometimes get so focused on the rituals of religion that I forget what your word says and what the real church is. Father I ask you to help me not to be caught up in religion but to study your word, meditate on it and spend ample time in prayer having open communication with you. I know your spirit is inside me Lord and I ask that you fill me up. I remove the cap that I have kept closed for so long and allow you to pour into me. Help me to live out the purpose you created me for and allow me to not stall or delay those things you command me to do. Help me to instead, do as you commanded eagerly and promptly Lord, Amen!

Strength

Overcome

The LORD is my rock, my fortress, and my savior; my God is my rock, in whom I find protection. He is my shield, the power that saves me, and my place of safety.
Psalms 18:2 (NLT)

Oh Lord I need your protection right now Father, for you are my shield, my rock and my strong tower. I come seeking you since I know you are the only one who can keep me safe from all things. I feel that my life is in a downward spiral right now and the enemy is using those around me to cause destruction in my life. Lord I am your willing servant, I ask you to keep me safe from all hurt, harm and danger. If it is your will for me to have to go through the torment that seems to be lurking ahead, please give me the strength to overcome and outlast the torment. I thank you now for all these things and seal this prayer in Jesus name, Amen!

SUBMISSION

Your Will Not My Will

Going a little ahead, he fell on his face, praying, "My Father, if there is any way, get me out of this. But please, not what I want. You, what do you want?"
Matthew 26:39 (MSG)

Lord I thank you that your son Jesus Christ made this statement because he could have easily decided not to take on the crucifixion which was his purpose in life. The fact that Jesus knew your will and still went through with it gives me courage to do your will despite my feelings or emotions. Knowing what your will is for me is not nearly as hard as fulfilling it, so Lord I seek your will today. From this day forth I choose your will over my own will. I know the seriousness and implications of this prayer; I also know my life would be in utter turmoil and meaningless if I had never accepted you into my life as my Lord and Savior. Amen!

Laying Flesh Down

*And anyone who believes in God's Son has eternal life.
Anyone who doesn't obey the Son will never experience
eternal life but remains under God's angry judgment."*
John 3:36 (NLT)

This scripture helped me realize that by living for my
flesh and for this world I am not obeying your Son.
When I do so, I am keeping myself from eternal life and
just waiting for your angry judgement. I am so grateful
you said if I confess with my mouth and believe in my
heart that your Son is Lord, and that He died for my sins
and rose with all power in his hands, that I will have
eternal life. I pray that people begin to open their hearts
to your word and that scriptures like this open their eyes
before it is too late. All they have to do is come to you
seeking your help and let you do the work in their life.
For I know if you can change me from where I was
before my walk with you then you can change anyone! I
know you are the ultimate makeover expert and I am so
grateful for all you have done for me Father. I thank you
now for everything you are going to do in my life and
seal this prayer in Jesus name, Amen!

TEMPTATION

People Pleasing

Obviously, I'm not trying to win the approval of people, but of God. If pleasing people were my goal, I would not be Christ's servant.
Galatians 1:10 (NLT)

Lord so many times in my life I have struggled with the issue of trying to please people and win their approval. I have also come to realize, whether I want to accept it or not, that trying to please others and win their approval will not fill the emotional void I have. The only person who can fill the void in my life and bring completeness is you Lord. Since I know you called me to walk the straight and narrow path, I already know I will find myself isolated from the "in crowd" at times. There will come a time when I have to reanalyze my relationships with friends and others, and cut off people who are keeping me from growing spiritually. This is a necessary move to help me be closer to you Lord; I am a slave to you forever and always. I declare your will, not my will Father! I thank you now for all these things and seal this prayer in Jesus name, Amen!

Temptation

Eye Gates

I have made a sacred pledge with my eyes. How then could I stare at a young woman with desire?
Job 31:1 (VOICE)

My conscience and my eyes are the contracting parties; you are the Judge. I am therefore bound not to look upon anything with a delighted or covetous eye. In doing so my conscience is defiled, but most importantly I am dishonoring you Lord. Please help me keep my covenant between you and my eyes so they will not cause me to bring you dishonor by sinning. I know that to overcome these temptations you will present certain situations to test my will. I pray right now that you help me to operate in my spirit at all times and prove that this contract has been permanently signed and sealed in my heart. I declare it so, in the name of Jesus Christ, Amen!

TRUST

Check the Unbelief

Blessed is the man who trusts in the Lord.
Jeremiah 17:7 (NLT)

Lord your word talks a lot about trusting and believing in you. One story from Mark 9:14-29 talks about a boy who was possessed by an impure spirit. The boy's father takes him to Jesus to get his son healed, but shows that he does not fully trust that Jesus can heal his son. Then the father asks Jesus to help him overcome his unbelief. I can sometimes get caught up in my unbelief when things seem too overwhelming for me. I pray for your help, but in the back of my mind doubt that you will do it. I know everything you have done for me, I know I do not deserve the grace and mercy you continue to give me. Sometimes I think I have used up all the grace and mercy you have for me. I know I do not always make Godly decisions when I should, which is what causes the manifestation of my doubts. Father please help me right now to trust you entirely with everything you have given me and with my entire life. Amen!

Through Good and Bad

And we know that God causes everything to work together for the good of those who love God and are called according to His purpose for them.
Romans 8:28 (NLT)

Lord I trust you with my life. I know it is easy for me to say this when life is going great and I am prospering, but Father I trust you right now even when my life seems to be flipped upside down and things are chaotic and in turmoil. I say this because I know you are true to your Word which declares that all things work together for my good. I love you and know that you have a plan and purpose for me which has not been fulfilled since I am still alive. So Lord I know regardless of how things seem to be going in my life, you see the entire puzzle and I am just focused on the individual pieces. I will stay rooted in faith knowing you allow everything to happen for my good. Amen!

Stop and Examine

You will keep the peace, a perfect peace, for all who trust in You, for those who dedicate their hearts and minds to You.
Isaiah 26:3 (VOICE)

Oh God, I sometimes contemplate in my head why things are not going right in my life and why I just cannot seem to obtain the peace you said I can have. I sometimes try to argue with you that I am doing all these things for you, and point out that yet my life is still in utter chaos. I realize now that the reason my life has not changed is because I am not completely dependent on you and I sometimes focus on my abilities and myself. Lord I come asking for your forgiveness. Please help me to fully trust you. I know it is only because of you that I am here today. So Lord today I am saying I trust you with my life, I declare your will, not my will anymore. Amen!

WITNESSING

Christ Like

I pray that from his glorious, unlimited resources he will empower you with inner strength through his Spirit. Then Christ will make his home in your hearts as you trust in him. Your roots will grow down into God's love and keep you strong...Now all glory to God, who is able, through his mighty power at work within us, to accomplish infinitely more than we might ask or think.
Ephesians 3:16-20 (NLT)

Lord, I ask right now that you allow people to understand the love of Christ and help me to be more of an example of what that looks like to this lost nation. I pray for those who specifically need to know the depths of Jesus' love; for he loved each of us so much that he willingly laid down his life. He took the most gruesome and humiliating form of punishment for a crime he didn't commit. Thank you Jesus for taking on my sins when you went to the cross and also taking my family's sin and this nation's sins. God I ask again that you help me to be a living example of what the love of Christ looks like so I can help bring those lost souls to you Lord. Amen!

Character

Show proper respect to everyone, love the family of believers, fear God, honor the emperor.
1 Peter 2:17

Father, keep me from damaging my home and my family, with the restraining power of your Holy Spirit, by not using careless, critical, or perilous words. Keep me from damaging my character and reputation when I am around my friends and coworkers, by operating in my spirit and not gossiping. Help me to be a living representative of Christ for everyone to see. Help me to focus on building people up instead of ripping them apart by attacking their flaws and faults. I want to honor you through my actions and words, so Lord I seek your strength to accomplish these things. Amen!

Evangelize

He asked the God of Israel, "Please bless me and extend my territory. Let Your hand be with me and guard me from harm so I will not experience pain as my mother did." And God did just that.
1 Chronicles 4:10 (VOICE)

Lord, I thank you for this scripture because it shows me that I can pray big. It shows me that if I pray with a sincere heart and it lines up with your will, then you will answer. So I pray right now that you help me to influence not only those I deal with on a day to day basis, but help me to reach people throughout the world. Help prepare me for greater things so I can go out to evangelize and witness to people of all races, genders, nationalities, religions, and sexual preferences. I pray that I will evoke a positive change and cause those people to give their lives to you Father. I want to help people get off the path of destruction they are currently on and get them on the straight and narrow path of righteousness. Amen!

Confession

Who is this King of glory? The Lord strong and mighty, the Lord mighty in battle. Lift up your heads, you gates; lift them up, you ancient doors, that the King of glory may come in.

Psalm 24:8-9

God, I know that confession is one of the hardest things for me to do and I find myself too ashamed to admit my sins and things that have a stronghold over my life. However, I also know that you are more than capable of breaking the chains and removing the strongholds in my life. Lord you are strong and mighty, you are undefeated in battle, and nothing can stand up against you. Lord I don't want to live my life according to Matthew 6:24, trying to serve two masters, so I humble myself before you, seeking only you. Take away all the darkness inside of me and fill me with your marvelous light. Allow my testimony to cause a shift in lives of those who are present; break the chains of bondage, and bring people out of the darkness and into your marvelous light. I thank you now for all these things and seal this prayer in Jesus name, Amen!

Spreading the Gospel

Do you need reminding that the unjust have no share in the blessings of the kingdom of God? Do not be misled...Some of you used to live in these ways, but you are different now; you have been washed clean, set apart, restored, and set on the right path in the name of the Lord Jesus, the Anointed, by the Spirit of our living God.
1 Corinthians 6:9-11 (VOICE)

At times I find myself focusing more on my own needs and not on the assignments you have given me. Lord I want more of you so I can reach more people outside of the ones I am in direct contact with. Allow my entire life to be used by you to touch the lives of people in the world. Lord I want to introduce multitudes of people to you so I can build up your Kingdom, and so they can receive your salvation. Help me not to get so caught up in my own desires but to look for opportunities to help someone every day so that I can share your love to them. Lord I know if I continue striving daily to help bring someone into your presence through my daily worship, then there will be a ripple effect of your light being spread. I want my worship and eagerness to serve you and to effectively bring a nation to you Father. Amen!

Witnessing

Being an Example

For God is not unjust. He will not forget how hard you have worked for him and how you have shown your love to him by caring for other believers, as you still do.
Hebrews 6:10 (NLT)

Lord, I thank you right now for your word because so many times I think my slip-ups will cause you to forget what I have done for you. Every day when I go to work I remember that I need to work as if I were doing it for you; like you are sitting at my desk or standing by my side supervising my performance. I know there are other people watching and I have heard all the talks at my job about those employees who do not do much work and those who work way too much. I want to be a Godly example for others at my job so they can see how great you are. Lord, help me to show my love for you by caring for other believers, but also for those who are lost or who have rejected you. In doing so I hope to exemplify the love your son Jesus Christ showed while he was here on earth and continues to show now. I thank you right now for these things Lord, until we speak again I just praise your wonderful name God. Amen!

WORDS

Actions vs. Words

Let us not love with words or tongue but with action and in truth.
1 John 3:18 (NLT)

Lord, I know the words of my mouth can be used to uplift and encourage or devastate and destroy, depending on how I use them. Like the saying goes "actions speak louder than words". Lord I ask that my actions speak for me and show that I live my life for you. I know I have made promises to you and others, and that the only way for those promises to be broken is if my actions do not back up my words. I ask for clear vision to see if and when my actions are beginning to get off so that I can realign my actions to what I have promised you and others. I thank you right now for helping me to keep and stay focused. Amen!

Encouragement

The tongue can bring death or life, those who love to talk will reap the consequences.
Proverbs 18:21 (NLT)

Lord, I know I struggle with allowing poison to come out of my mouth when I put people down, talk harshly to them and show disrespectful behavior towards them. Lord, I am sorry for the hurtful things I have allowed to come off my tongue and out of my mouth. I ask right now that you change my thinking and communication to reflect the love you have given me. I know there have been plenty of times when you could have and should have written me off, yet you kept on loving me in spite of my transgressions and iniquities. Help me to speak love and encouragement over people and in doing so it will allow them to experience your love and open their hearts to you Lord. Amen!

Name of Jesus

Then Jesus said, "Come to me, all of you who are weary and carry heavy burdens, and I will give you rest."
Matthew 11:28 (NLT)

Lord, thank you for your son Jesus Christ; by calling on his name I know that I am no longer alone. I know that my sorrows, pains and frustrations will be removed and replaced with the peace, strength, and love of Jesus. At times I do not truly acknowledge the power of saying that name "Jesus". For it is written in your Word that the lame begin to walk and the sick are healed due to the power of saying his great name. Demons are cast out of individuals and the dead are raised to life when they are commanded to do so in the name of Jesus. I am so thankful for the power that is in the name of "Jesus Christ". I feel chains being broken and weights being removed right now just shouting and declaring the powerful name…Jesus! Thank you Jesus, Amen!

Lock It Up

*An offended friend is harder to win back than a fortified
city. Arguments separate friends like a gate locked with bars.*
Proverbs 18:19 (NLT)

God please help me to keep my words minimal and keep
a lock on my mouth to prevent things from spewing out
that I will later regret. Help me to process my words
before letting them freely flow out unfiltered. I don't
want my emotions to control my life and the words of
my mouth. Lord, I ask you to help the words of my
mouth line up with your perfect will and ways. I don't
want things released from my mouth that go against your
will or give a bad example of me living a life for Christ.
Just as water reflects the face; so one's life reflects the
heart. So Lord please keep my heart pure and softened to
your word and your will so I can be more conscious of
what I allow out of my mouth. Amen!

Purpose over Emotions

Pleasant words are like a honeycomb: they drip sweet food
for life and bring health to the body.
Proverbs 16:24 (VOICE)

Lord you know watching what I say is a difficult task for me; so many times situations come up that cause me to react out of my flesh. I say words that I wish later I had never let spew from my mouth. I get so caught up in my emotions and feelings that I lose focus on my destiny and purpose. Regardless of how others treat me I am still supposed to show them respect and Godly love. So Lord please help me to keep my words kind so you can use my words to be the honey to someone else's soul and help encourage them. I no longer want others to change my behavior or attitude; I want your spirit inside of me to change them by my words; allow them to experience the love of Jesus. Amen!